Walk Around

By LOU DRENDEL

P-40 Warhawk

Walk Around Number 8

squadron/signal publications

INTRODUCTION

The P-40 was one of the most important fighters of World War II. Although it's performance did not compare to other fighters of the day, the P-40 was used successfully on all fronts. P-40 production lasted for five years, during which 13,737 were produced. In 1941 and 1942, some 6,699 P-40s were manufactured, compared to 1,469 P-38s, 2,898 P-39s, 531 P-47s, and 767 P-51s. The P-40 was a bargain for the taxpayers. Production cost of the P-40N was $52,869, while the P-38 averaged $126, 234, the P-39 $71,965, the P-47 $114, 377, and the P-51 $64,872.

The P-40 was flown by most allied air forces. It was one of the most important fighters of the British and Commonwealth forces in Africa and Asia. It was also the the mount of the legendary "Flying Tigers", the American Volunteer Group, China's who helped defend China against the Imperial Japanese Air Force. The majority of the detail photos in this Walk Around are of one of the best warbird restorations in this country. Dick Hansen's recreation of the P-40E flown by General Robert L. Scott, commander of the 23rd Fighter Group, successors to the Tigers.

Also covered in much less detail is the Curtiss Hawk 75. The Hawk was the progenitor of the P-40, in line and in name with all P-40 variants, foreign or domestic, were named with some Hawk variation, "Warhawk, Kittyhawk, Tomahawk". All of the photos and detail drawings of the Hawk contained herein are from original Curtiss Wright manuals.

The Curtiss Hawk 75 was designed in 1934, and flown for the first time in 1935. Engine problems, however, delayed its introduction until 1937, when Curtiss received the largest peacetime order for a fighter ever placed. The Army Air Corps placed an order for 210 P-36As, worth $4,113,550, on 7 July 1937.

The decade from 1935 to 1945 was one of tremendous growth and vitality for American aeronautics. The impending war injected a sense of purpose and new designs flowed from the best engineering minds in the country. While it was designed to be the USAAC's modern fighter, it was already slated for replacement by the P-40. Pilots who flew the P-36 were enthusiastic about its handling and maneuverability, so it should have been no surprise that the more powerful Allison V-1710 liquid-cooled in-line engine would become the definitive power plant for the Hawk airframe which became the P-40.

The 10th production P-36A was equipped with an Allison V-1710, and flown as the XP-40 on 14 October 1938. The XP-40 competed with the XP-38, XP-39, and Seversky AP-4 in the Air Corps sponsored competition at Wright Field on 25 January 1939, emerging as the clear winner. Further improvements to the design resulted in another "largest contract since WW I" in April 1939, when Curtiss was awarded a contract for 542 P-40s. Our P-40 Walk Around will illustrate several types of P-40, but the main detailed study will concentrate on the P-40E.

Acknowledgements

This is my first effort at producing a book on a Second World War aircraft. As a dedicated member of the Experimental Aircraft Association and its Warbirds Of America division, I have seen and photographed many of the great restorations of Second World War aircraft, but my preoccupation with modern military aircraft left me at a loss when it came to providing photographic coverage of WW II aircraft. Fortunately, my long-time friend and contributor, Norm Taylor, came to the rescue with several nice war time shots of P-40s. Another long-time friend and fellow Squadron/Signal author, Jim Sullivan, opened his archives.

ISBN 0-89747-361-2

If you have any photographs of aircraft, armor, soldiers or ships of any nation, particularly wartime snapshots, why not share them with us and help make Squadron/Signal's books all the more interesting and complete in the future. Any photograph sent to us will be copied and the original returned. The donor will be fully credited for any photos used. Please send them to:

Squadron/Signal Publications, Inc.
1115 Crowley Drive
Carrollton, TX 75011-5010

Если у вас есть фотографии самолётов, вооружения, солдат или кораблей любой страны, особенно, снимки времен войны, поделитесь с нами и помогите сделать новые книги издательства Эскадрон/Сигнал еще интереснее. Мы переснимем ваши фотографии и вернём оригиналы. Имена приславших снимки будут сопровождать все опубликованные фотографии. Пожалуйста, присылайте фотографии по адресу:

Squadron/Signal Publications, Inc.
1115 Crowley Drive
Carrollton, TX 75011-5010

軍用機、装甲車両、兵士、軍艦などの写真を所持しておられる方はいらっしゃいませんか？どの国のものでも結構です。作戦中に撮影されたものが特に良いのです。Squadron/Signal社の出版する刊行物において、このような写真は内容を一層充実し、興味深くすることができます。当方にお送り頂いた写真は、複写の後お返しいたします。出版物中に写真を使用した場合は、必ず提供者のお名前を明記させて頂きます。お写真は下記にご送付ください。

Squadron/Signal Publications, Inc.
1115 Crowley Drive
Carrollton, TX 75011-5010

Dick Hansen and Rudy Frasca allowed me free rein to photograph their restored P-40Es. During an airshow appearance at Fort Lauderdale, I was fortunate to make the acquaintance of a friendly FAA inspector. Walt Houghton is a dedicated enthusiast and collector, and he was kind enough to lend me his P-40 memorabilia, which included P-36 and P-40 tech manuals and photography which had belonged to his cousin, Paul Carpenter. Carpenter was with Curtiss-Wright from the mid-30s throughout the Second World War, as a tech rep to combat units and finally Assistant Service Manager.

Owner Dick Hansen, in period costume, flies his magnificent P-40E Warhawk restoration, painted as General Robert L. Scott's fighter, over the fall fields of Northern Illinois, during 1994. (Lou Drendel)

One of the light weight, fixed landing gear Hawk 75-O demonstrators was purchased by the Argentine Air Force during 1938. Argentina received twenty from Curtiss and also assembled another thirty Hawk 75-Os under license, retaining them in service as fighter trainers with 1 Grupo de Caca at El Plumerillo Air Base well into the early 1950s. The fixed gear Hawk 75s, were intended as light weight, easy to maintain fighters for smaller air forces. Besides Argentina, they were flown by China (Hawk 75H demonstator and Hawk 75M and Siam (Thailand [Hawk 75N]). (Curtiss via Walt Houghton)

Installation of the 875 hp Wright GR-1820-G3 Cyclone air cooled radial engine in a Hawk 75-O. The engine used two exhaust collector rings which fed exhaust into two exhaust stacks that protruded from the lower engine cowling. The stacks were covered by large streamlined fairings.

CURTISS HAWK 75-O

3

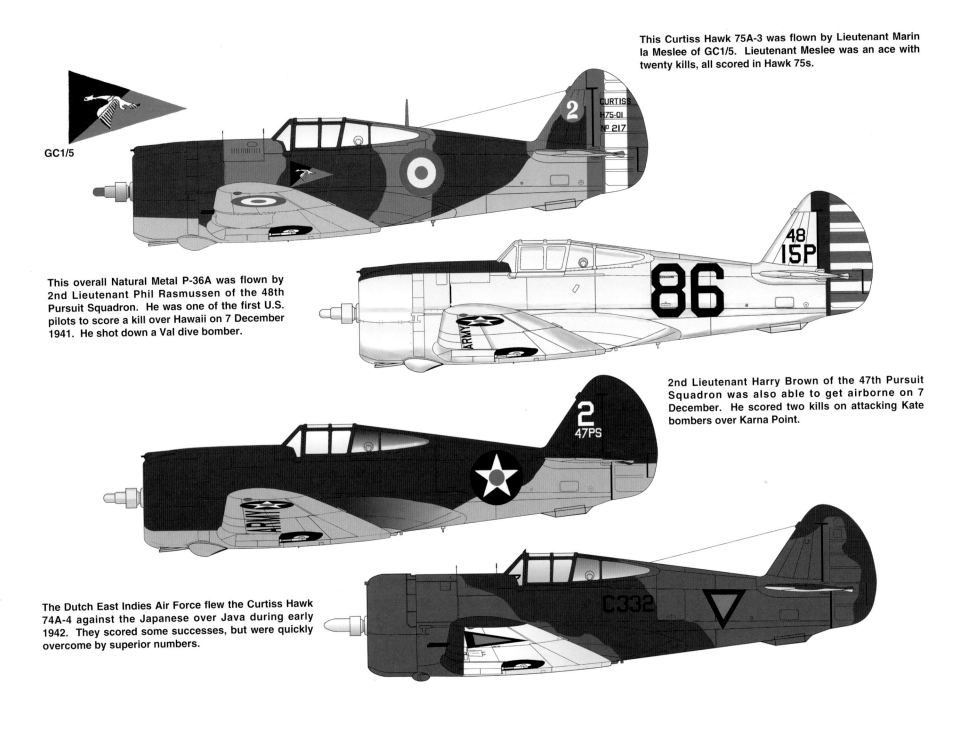

This Curtiss Hawk 75A-3 was flown by Lieutenant Marin la Meslee of GC1/5. Lieutenant Meslee was an ace with twenty kills, all scored in Hawk 75s.

GC1/5

This overall Natural Metal P-36A was flown by 2nd Lieutenant Phil Rasmussen of the 48th Pursuit Squadron. He was one of the first U.S. pilots to score a kill over Hawaii on 7 December 1941. He shot down a Val dive bomber.

2nd Lieutenant Harry Brown of the 47th Pursuit Squadron was also able to get airborne on 7 December. He scored two kills on attacking Kate bombers over Karna Point.

The Dutch East Indies Air Force flew the Curtiss Hawk 74A-4 against the Japanese over Java during early 1942. They scored some successes, but were quickly overcome by superior numbers.

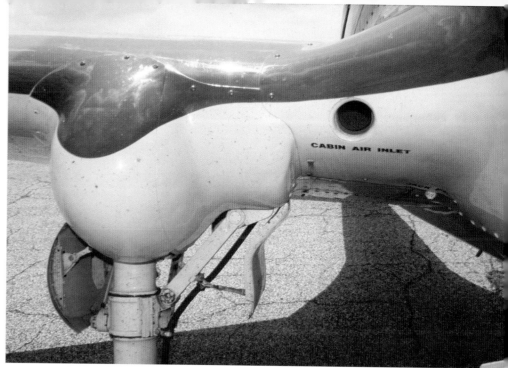

The right main gear wing leading edge fairing on the P-40E was also the same as used on the earlier P-36 series. (Lou Drendel)

The main gear wheel well on a P-40E. The wing leading edge is to the left, the trailing edge is to the right, where the flap demarkation line is visible. (Lou Drendel)

Right main gear of the P-40E. The Hawk 75A and P-36 used the same retractable main landing gear as the follow-on P-40 series, although the arrangement of the landing gear doors was different. The P-36 series had the door attached to the landing gear strut, while the P-40 series have the doors on the wing. (Lou Drendel)

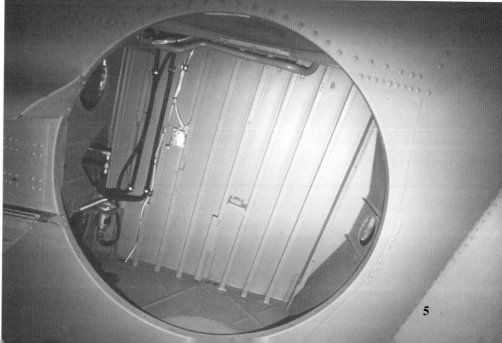

Curtiss P-36C

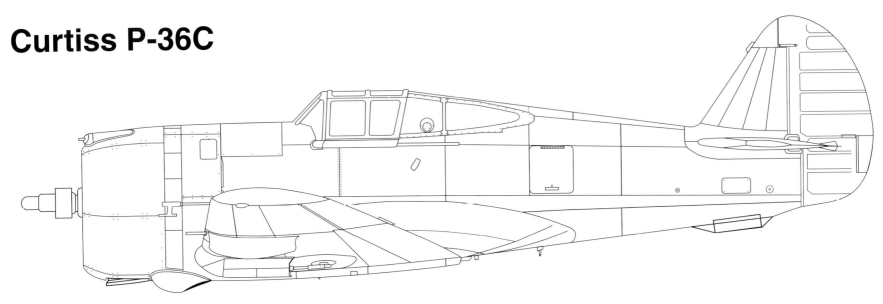

The right side of the Hawk 75-O cockpit contains the canopy hand crank, map case, oxygen regulator, very pistol, pilot's helmet and flap controls. All the cockpit lettering was in Spanish. (Curtiss via Walt Houghton)

The P-36C differed from the light weight fixed gear Hawk 75s in that it had a more powerful engine and retractable landing gear.

The left side of the Hawk 75-O cockpit contained holders for ten signal flares, a fire extinguisher, the throttle, propeller and mixture controls, bomb hand release, elevator and rudder trim wheels and main electrical panel. (Curtiss via Walt Houghton)

Tablero de instrumentos y controles cabina del piloto
CURTISS HAWK 75-0
INSTRUMENT BOARD
S-F 11463   11-15-38.

The Hawk 75-O main instrument panel. Conspicuous by its absence is an electric artificial horizon. Instrument flying in the Hawk was truly needle, ball, and airspeed. The cutouts in the upper left and right corners of the panel were for the breechs of the two cowling mounted .30 caliber Madsen M-1935 machine guns. (Curtiss via Walt Houghton)

The fixed main landing gear, with the oleo strut compressed (weight on gear), of a Hawk 75-O. A streamlined fairing and full wheel pants were added to improve the aircraft's aerodynamics and cut down on drag. (Curtiss via Walt Houghton)

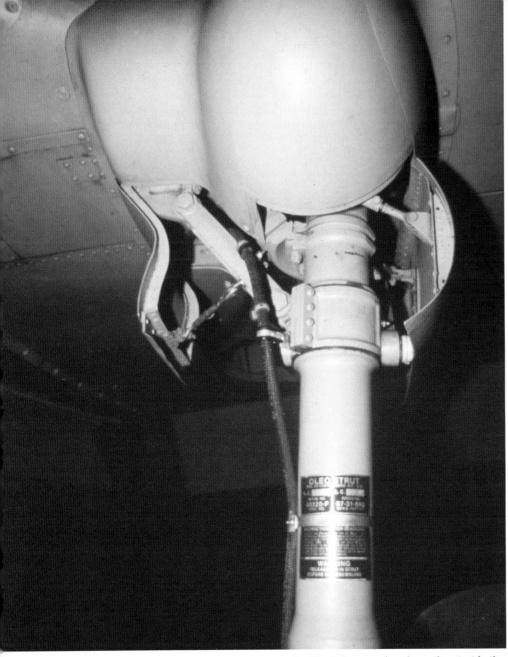

The port main gear strut, looking to the rear. The Black line running down the strut is the hydraulic line for the brakes. Also visible is the side strut which is attached to the inner landing gear door. At the top of the side strut is the strut hinge block. (Lou Drendel)

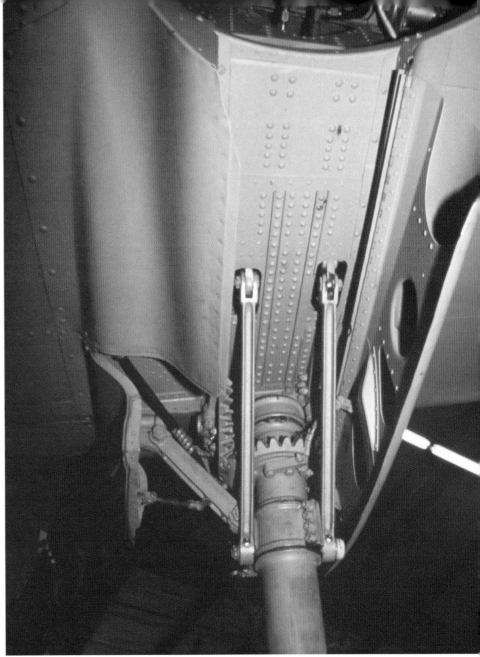

P-40E port main gear strut, looking forward. The main gear rotates 90 degrees, allowing the wheel to lay flat in the main gear well. The two struts extending up into the wing are the lower retracting links, which attach to the retracting arm located inside the wing. The vertical set of gears are the bevel gear, while the horizontal gear is the pinion gear. (Lou Drendel)

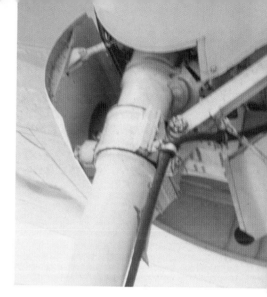

P-40E starboard main landing gear detals, including the side strut. Not all P-40s used a main landing gear wheel cover. (Lou Drendel)

Inboard view of P-40E port main gear. The oleo scissor is the V shaped assembly behind the wheel. The Black line is the hydraulic brake line. The shiney area is the oleo piston. (Lou Drendel)

The main gear strut of the Hawk 75-O, with the oleo fully extended. The aircraft used a smooth treadless tire. The Black line running from the underside of the wing, down the landing gear leg to the wheel was the hydraulic line for the brake. (Curtiss via Walt Houghton)

Rear fuselage interior of a Hawk 75-O, showing the radio sets (6, 7, 8, 9) and the two flare ejection tubes (5) which were controlled via two toggle handles on the lower right side of the cockpit sidewall. (Curtiss via Walt Houghton)

The Hawk 75-O could mount a gun camera above the cowling in front of the cockpit to record gun fire or for training. (Curtiss via Walt Houghton)

An alternative fuselage gun installation used electrical gun chargers, rather than the manual system. (Curtiss via Walt Houghton)

The Hawk 75-O mounted two .30 caliber machine guns in the fuselage. In this gun installation the weapons were manually charged by the pilot using the handle at the rear of the gun. (Curtiss via Walt Houghton)

The right side of the fuselage gun installation. In addition to the two cowl guns, the Hawk 75-0 also had two .30 caliber guns in each wing. (Curtiss via Walt Houghton)

11

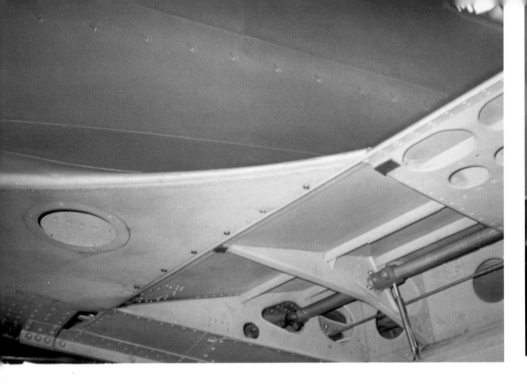

The P-40E uses hydraulically operated split flaps. These are the starboard flaps in the fully extended position, revealing the interior ribbing and push-pull actuating rods. The aileron control cables run through the holes in the uper wing ribbing. One of the aileron control cable adjustment turnbuckles is visible in the foreground (below left). The holes in the forward bulkhead are lightening holes designed to lessen the overall weight of the aircraft. (Lou Drendel)

This restored P-40E carries the markings of Colonel Robert L. Scott. The aircraft differs from wartime P-40Es in that it has the late style exhaust stacks and has a radio antenna mast on the fuselage behind the cockpit. Wartime P-40Es had antenna wires running from the fin tip to each wing tip. (Lou Drendel)

The original production model of the P-40 retained the two fuselage mounted .50 caliber machine guns and had a single .30 caliber machine gun in each wing. The large air scoop on top of the cowling was the carburetor air intake, with the machine gun fairings on either side. (Norm Taylor Collection)

A P-40B of the 77th Pursuit Squadron, 20th Pursuit Group on the ramp at Oakland, California during August of 1941. (Pete Bowers via Norman E. Taylor)

This P-40B was assigned to the 55th Pursuit Squadron, 35th Pursuit Group, based at Hamilton Field, California during January of 1940. (Pete Bowers via Norman E. Taylor)

Camouflaged P-40Bs of the 33rd Pursuit Squadron share the ramp at Bellows Field, Hawaii with Natural Metal B-18s, B-17s and a single P-36. The P-40s were Olive Drab over Neutral Gray, with Yellow numbers and full rudder stripes. The squadron insignia was carried on the fuselage. (Norm Taylor collection)

A P-40C of the 33rd Pursuit Squadron, Iceland on 23 September, 1941. The P-40C was the first variant to be able to carry an under fuselage fuel tank, plus having an increased internal fuel capacity. (Norm Taylor collection)

Armorers boresight the nose and wing guns on a P-40B of the 19th Fighter Squadron at Bellows Field, Hawaii during 1942. The P-40B carried two .50 caliber guns in the nose and four .30 caliber machine guns in the wings. The propeller was Natural Metal. (Norm Taylor collection)

A P-40B of the 33rd Pursuit Squadron. P-40Bs had self-sealing fuel tanks, pilot armor and an armored windscreen. The B also had provision for underwing bomb racks. (Dave Menard via Norm Taylor collection)

15

The starboard wing flap in the fully extended position, looking outboard. The actuating hydraulic line has been disconnected from the main hydraulic supply in the fuselage. The cables running through the flaps are the aileron control cables. (Lou Drendel)

When the flaps are deployed, a small Red post extends from the wing to visually let the pilot know that the flaps are down. This restored P-40N has a Black non-skid walk way on the wing root area. (Nick Waters)

Visible on the underside of the starboard wing, looking outboard are the open gun bay door, a portion of the wheel well, a section of the lowered flap, and the alieron. The interior of the gun bay was painted in Zinc Chromate Green primer, while the wheel well is the same color as the surrounding wing surface. (Lou Drendel)

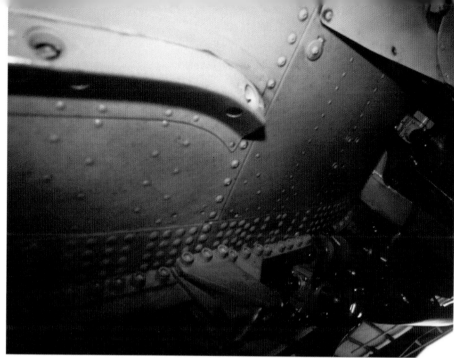

(Above/Below) The underside of forward fuselage, just behind the engine bay. The engine cooling cowl flaps are in the full closed position, normally used when the aircraft is in flight. For engine start and run-up on the ground, the cowl flaps would be in the fully open position to allow as much cooling air through the radiators as possible. (Lou Drendel)

The retractable P-40E tailwheel, looking aft. The wheel retraction mechanism is protected by a canvas boot that keeps out dust, dirt and debris. The wheel retracts to the rear, with the wheel well being covered by a pair of doors. The tail wheel tire is a smooth, treadless type tire. (Lou Drendel)

Ground crewmen perform routine engine maintenance on an RAF Tomahawk in the Western African Desert. (Paul Carpenter via Walt Houghton)

A RAF Tomahawk up on home made jacks during an overhaul at a maintenance facility in Egypt. The four wing guns have been removed. Part of the maintenance procedure was a drop check of the landing gear. (Paul Carpenter via Walt Houghton)

Tail wheel detail of a P-40E. The retractable tail wheel has a canvas cover around the upper mechanism to keep out dirt and debris. The tailwheel itself mounted a smooth treadless tire. (Lou Drendel)

The right main landing gear well and under fuselage center section of a P-40E. There is an electrical conduit running through the wheel well to a junction box. (Lou Drendel)

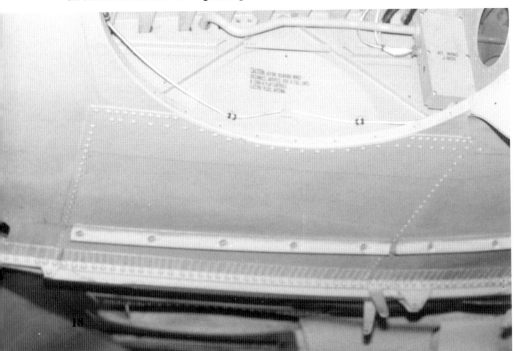

An early P-40 moves down the Curtiss assembly line on a four wheeled dolly. The inside of the wheel well was canvas, which could be opened to gain access to the interior of the wing. (via Larry Davis)

These are the fuel tank supports and bomb sway braces on a P-40E. (James Roeder)

Curtiss workers perform check-outs on P-40Bs on the open ramp at the Curtiss plant. The aircraft at right is having its gun sight aligned for the twin nose guns. (via Larry Davis)

These P-40Bs are in various stages of final assembly/check out at the Curtiss plant. The Red dot in the national insignia indicates that the time period was either pre-war or very early in the war. (via Larry Davis)

Underside of a P-40E, showing the installation of the 52 gallon drop tank and engine cowl flaps in the full open position. The drop tank is secured in place on the centerline bomb rack, and supported by four sway braces, two on each side. The tube forward of the rack is the fuel intake tube, which fed fuel from the drop tank, through a strainer, to the fuselage fuel tank. (Lou Drendel)

The port P-40E engine cooling cowl flaps. These flaps are controlled by the pilot and used to augment cooling at slower speeds and when running the engine on the ground. The small air intake feeds cooling air to the engine crankcase. (Lou Drendel)

The actuating rod for the cowl flaps is visible above the top flap. There are a total of four segments all of which operate as a single unit. (Lou Drendel)

(Right) The rear side of the engine cooling cowl flaps. The two actuating rods move the flaps in and out, with the two side flaps being tied into the main center flaps by connecting rods. (Nick Waters)

87-66-522
PANEL DISCONNECT BOX

87-64-004
WING FLAP
ACTUATING CYLINDER

87-06-528
CENTER LINE
BULKHEAD

87-66-521
PANEL DISCONNECT BOX

WING PANELS SEPARATED

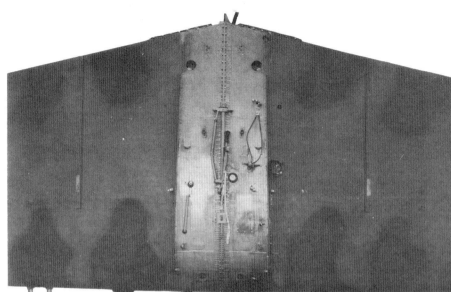

WING PANEL - TOP & BOTTOM VIEW

22

A P-40N-20-CU (43-23977) built for the Chinese Air Force, chocked down on the ramp at the Curtiss factory on 23 December 1943. A Curtiss C-46 Commando is in the background. (Roger Besecker via Norm Taylor Collection)

A rather war-weary P-40E of the 8th Fighter Squadron, 49th Fighter Group at Eagle Pass Army Air Field, Texas, during the Summer of 1944. It was on loan to the T-6 pilot training base and was used to give fledgling cadets their first taste of fighter flying. (Bill Reynolds via Norm Taylor collection)

Rudy Frasca's P-40E carries the markings of the Panda Bear Squadron of the American Volunteer Group (AVG) "Flying Tigers." The Tigers did not receive P-40Es until March of 1942, and were absorbed into the USAAF a short time later, becoming known as the China Air Task Force, under the command of General Chennault. (Lou Drendel)

The split air intake directs airflow to the triple radiators housed within the scoop. Like the Hansen restoration, this P-40E also uses the late style exhaust stacks. (Lou Drendel)

AVG Panda Bear squadron insignia on Frasca's P-40E. The gloss camouflage finish is not authentic, but it is long-lasting. This P-40 is part of the Frasca Museum of flying war-birds, which is headquartered in Urbana, Illinois,. The Museum also also includes a Wildcat, Spitfire, T-6, T-34, Stearman and, under restoration, a Fiat. (Lou Drendel)

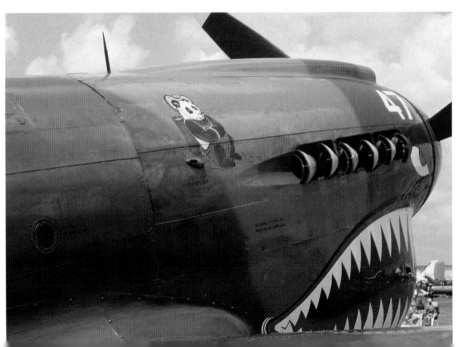

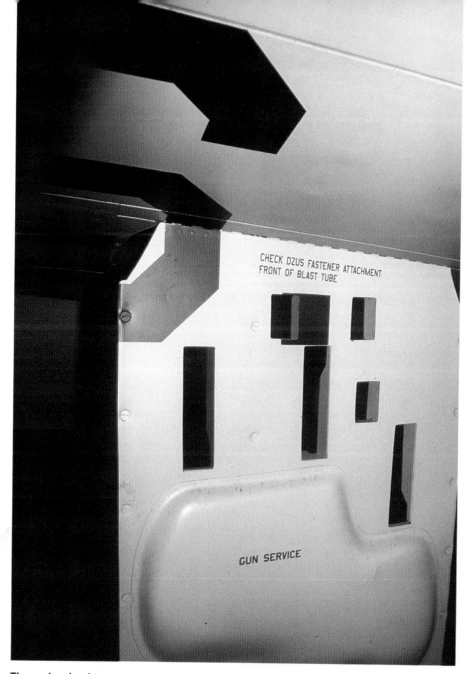

The underwing lower access door for the wing gun bay swings down to allow access to the bay. The holes in the door are the ejection port for empty shell casings, which are ejected overboard rather than retained. (Lou Drendel)

CHECK DZUS FASTENER ATTACHMENT
FRONT OF BLAST TUBE

GUN SERVICE

The underside of port wing houses a retractable landing light. The light is hinged on the forward side and swings down. Its use is controlled by the pilot. (Lou Drendel)

LET	NAME
A	REAR WING TANK GAGE
B	REAR WING TANK FILLER NECK
C	BALL & SOCKET JOINT ACCESS DOOR
D	AILERON CONTROL DRUM ACCESS DOOR
E	WHEEL POCKET INSTALLATION
F	COVER-GUN ADJUSTMENT LUGS
G	INSPECTION DOOR
H	HYDRAULIC LINES CUTOUT
I	FRESH AIR INLET
J	SUMP CUTOUT L.H. ONLY
K	LANDING GEAR FAIRING
L	LEADING EDGE COVER PLATE
M	CUTOUT-CAMERA CABLE
N	BOMB RACK COVER PLATE
O	INSPECTION DOOR
P	GUN ACCESS DOOR
Q	WHEEL POCKET INSTALLATION
R	FUEL TANK DOORS
S	AILERON BELLCRANK HOLES
T	FLAP ACTUATING CYLINDER ACCESS

STATIONS AND
ACCESS DOORS- WING

RIGHT & LEFT PANELS ARE IDENTICAL
EXCEPT AS NOTED.

UPPER SURFACE

LOWER SURFACE

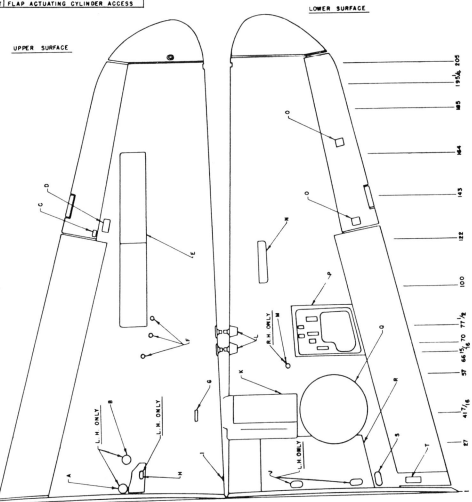

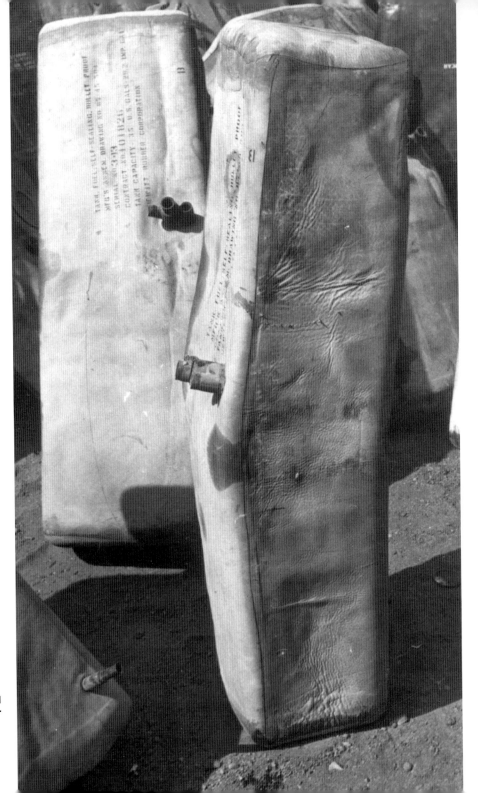

(Left) P-40 self-sealing fuel cells. The P-40 was equipped with two wing fuel tanks and one fuselage tank which gave it an internal fuel capacity of 149 gallons. (Paul Carpenter via Walt Houghton)

Lend-Lease P-40s arrived from the Curtiss plant in Buffalo in these wooden crates. They were shipped via sea to their various assembly points around the world where Curtiss tech reps would assist in reassembling the fighters. (Paul Carpenter via Walt Houghton)

P-40 wings used (and abused) await attachment at the theatre maintenance depot. After they were reassembled and test flown, the fighters would then be ferried to an operational unit. (Paul Carpenter via Walt Houghton)

Curtiss Tech Rep Paul Carpenter inspects a newly arrived P-40 in the Western Desert, while assigned to No. 2 Squadron, South African Air Force, 1942. (Paul Carpenter via Walt Houghton)

The open door to the fuselage compartment. The data case on the inside of the door was for log books, etc. and the first aid kit is on the underside of the hatch. This compartment also contained oxygen, radios, and hydraulic reservoirs. (Lou Drendel)

The Hansen P-40 has the control locks stored in the fuselage compartment (in Red). The hydraulic reservoir is visible forward of the locks. (Lou Drendel)

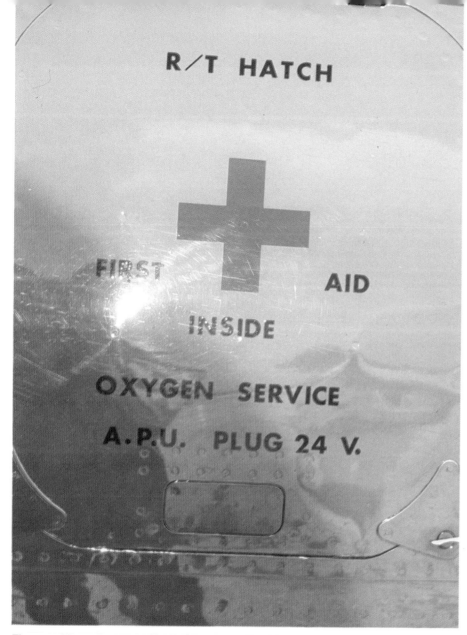

The stenciling on the door of the fuselage compartment of the P-40E restored by Frasca indicates that the push in door on the lower portion of the hatch is for the ground power unit plug-in. All stenciling was in Black (Lou Drendel)

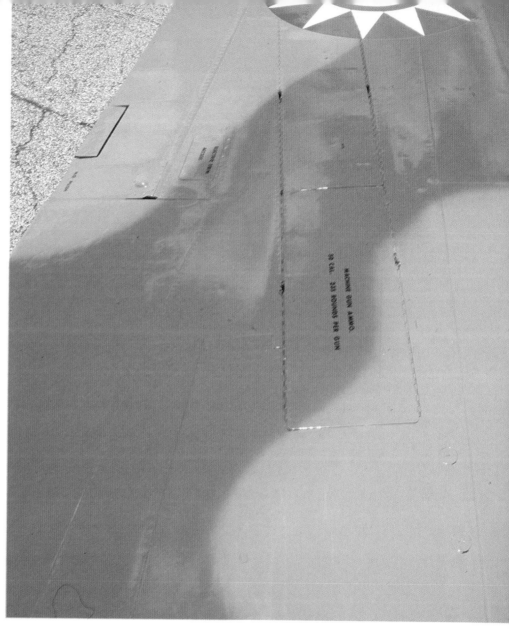

The upper wing surface of a P-40E contained the access doors for the gun ammunition bays. Belted .50 caliber machine gun ammunition for the three wing guns was loaded into the bay from above. Also visible are the aileron and the aileron trim tab. Just above the aileron is a small access panel, this is the aileron control drum access door. (Lou Drendel)

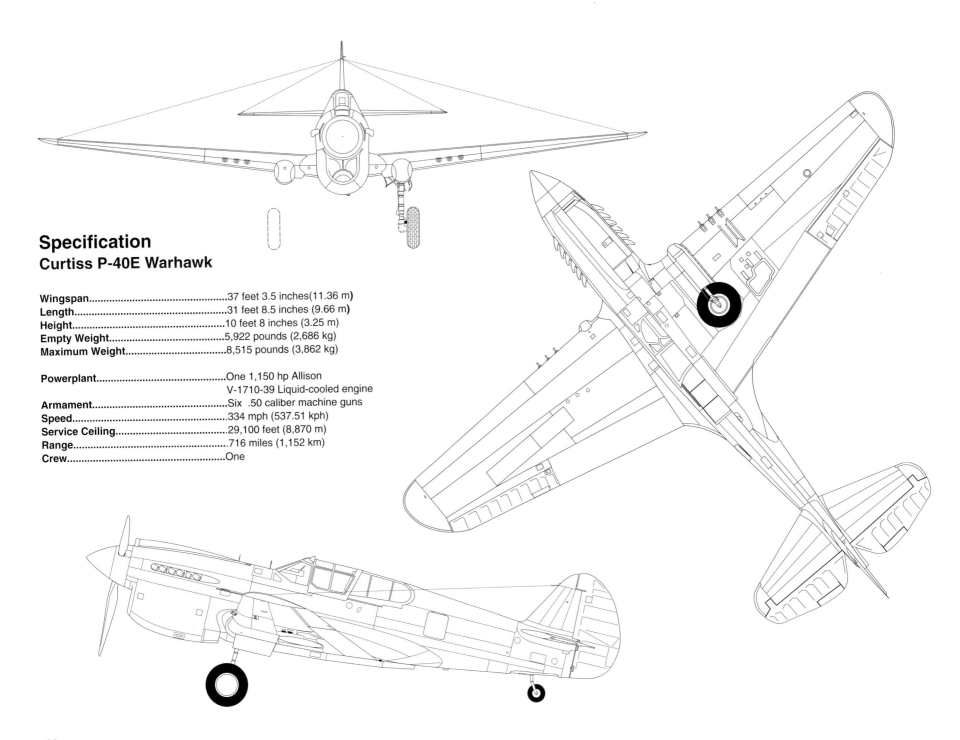

Specification
Curtiss P-40E Warhawk

Wingspan..37 feet 3.5 inches(11.36 m**)**
Length..31 feet 8.5 inches (9.66 m**)**
Height..10 feet 8 inches (3.25 m)
Empty Weight.......................................5,922 pounds (2,686 kg)
Maximum Weight..................................8,515 pounds (3,862 kg)

Powerplant...One 1,150 hp Allison
                              V-1710-39 Liquid-cooled engine
Armament...Six .50 caliber machine guns
Speed..334 mph (537.51 kph)
Service Ceiling......................................29,100 feet (8,870 m)
Range..716 miles (1,152 km)
Crew...One

P-40 Major Components

This P-40M was restored by the Lone Star Flight Museum and painted to represent a RAF Kittyhawk Mk III. The P-40M was equipped with an Allison V-1710-81 engine and had a longer fuselage than the P-40E. The aircraft was on display at Harrison, Arkansas during September of 1994. (Lou Drendel)

The camouflage colors on the Lone Star Flight Museum's P-40 are inaccurate. The sharkmouth was carried by No 112 Squadron of the Desert Air Force (squadron ID code GA) and the camouflage was Sand and Midstone uppersurfaces over Sky Blue undersurfaces. The fuselage band was a ID marking carried on fighters based in England, not in the desert. (Lou Drendel)

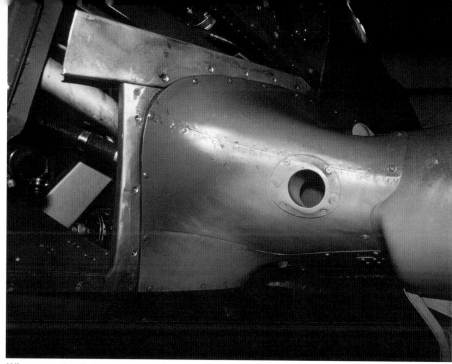

Wing root detail of the P-40E, showing the cabin fresh air intake, which supplies outside air to the cockpit. (Lou Drendel)

Fuselage center section of the Hansen restoration. The P-40E has the fuselage compartment lettering in Red against the national insignia. The upper line reads "First Aid Inside Door", the bottom line reads "Latch Before Flight." There are two small antennas visible under the fuselage for modern avionics systems. (Lou Drendel)

P-40E rear fuselage with open access/inspection panels. This is the P-40 restored by Hansen, which carries its civil registration number in small Black letters/numbers under the horizontal stabilizer. The object above the large open access/inspection panel is a blade antenna for modern avionics. (Lou Drendel)

This P-40E-1-CU on the ramp at the Curtiss factory had large drop tanks installed under the wings to test the concept of using them to ferry fighters across the Pacific and Atlantic Oceans. The advent of the escort carrier, which was used to ferry fighters to operational areas, made this modification unnecessary. (Roger Besecker via Norm Taylor collection)

Nose detail of a P-40F of the 85th Fighter Squadron, 79th Fighter Group in North Africa. The F model had a Rolls Royce engine, which eliminated the need for the carburetor air scoop on top of the cowl. The use of this engine also changed the location of the cowl flaps to a more forward position. (Norm Taylor collection)

The maintenance depot in Alexandria, Egypt was kept busy overhauling and repairing combat damaged P-40s from units in the western desert. (Paul Carpenter via Walt Houghton)

Three RAF Kittyhawk fuselage sections await overhaul at the rear area maintenance depot in Alexandria, Egypt. The aircraft in the foreground was from 260 Squadron. (Paul Carpenter via Walt Houghton)

A RAF mechanic repairs damage to the wing of a P-40. The wing center section skinning has been removed, exposing the wing self-sealing fuel cells. (Paul Carpenter via Walt Houghton)

The Hansen P-40E restoration was on display at the Experimental Aircraft Association fly-in at Oshkosh during 1995. (Lou Drendel)

The right aileron trim tab on the Hansen P-40E. Unlike the rudder and elevator trim tabs, which are cockpit controlled, this tab is ground adjustable only. Setting is through the trial and error method. There are two inspection plates, one on the tab and one on the elevator. (Lou Drendel)

Underside of the starboard reveals the placement of the national insignia and the position of the underside navigation light. (Lou Drendel)

The vertical fin and rudder of the P-40E has a cut out for the elevator hinge to pass through. The rudder trim tab control is protected by a streamlined cover and was controlled by the pilot via a trim wheel in the cockpit. (Lou Drendel)

The rear fuselage with all inspection panels secured in place. The small plate low on the fuselage was the lift point for raising the tail (normally done when bore-sighting the machine guns). (Lou Drendel)

Internal Arrangement

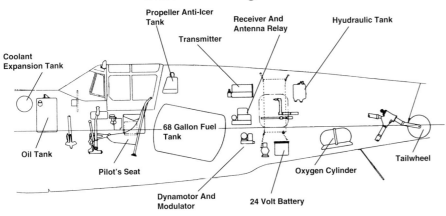

Coolant Expansion Tank

Oil Tank

Propeller Anti-Icer Tank

Transmitter

Pilot's Seat

68 Gallon Fuel Tank

Receiver And Antenna Relay

Hyudraulic Tank

Dynamotor And Modulator

24 Volt Battery

Oxygen Cylinder

Tailwheel

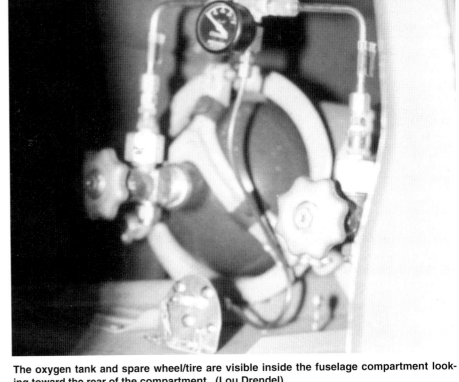

The oxygen tank and spare wheel/tire are visible inside the fuselage compartment looking toward the rear of the compartment. (Lou Drendel)

The circular inspection plate on the lower left fuselage has been removed to show the rudder cables. Also visible are two of the rudder hinge points. (Lou Drendel)

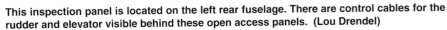

This inspection panel is located on the left rear fuselage. There are control cables for the rudder and elevator visible behind these open access panels. (Lou Drendel)

The stenciling on the fuselage alongside the baggage compartment is in Black and identifies some of the items that can be accessed or are stored in the compartment. (Lou Drendel)

The underside of elevator with the stick in the full nose-down position. The indent at the left is the elevator hinge balance. (Lou Drendel)

The elevator trim tab is controlled by the pilot by a wheel in the cockpit (the tab actuating rod is visible at the left.) Trim tabs are used to lighten control pressure and/or adjust pitch, roll, or yaw. The warning on the tab is in Black. (Lou Drendel)

Rudder trim tab and elevator spar pass-through. One of the main visual differences between the P-40E and later, longer-fuselage variants (P-40L, M, N) is that the elevator was located forward of the rudder hinge line on the long fuselage variants. The hands off warning was intended to prevent ground crewmen from bending or otherwise damaging the tab. (Lou Drendel)

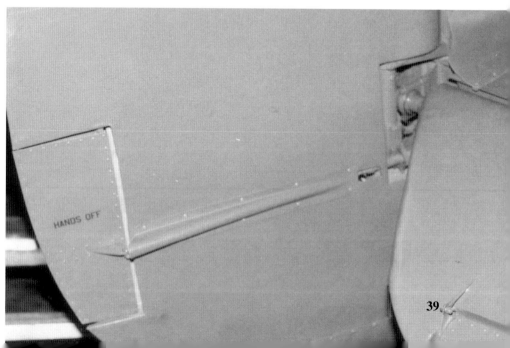

The hydraulic system vent and fuselage fuel tank drain are located on the fuselage underside just below the wing root. (Lou Drendel)

The pilot of this P-40E has left the shoulder harness straps hanging over the canopy railing. The straps were made of canvas and the headrest was covered in Brown leather. P-40E. The no step warning marking on the wing fillet is in Red, as are other caution/warning markings. (Lou Drendel)

Dzus fastners are used on the cowling and other access panels to allow quick removal/replacement. The object on the upper fuselage is the ring gun sight, which was used in conjunction with a post sight mounted further forward on the nose. (Lou Drendel)

The starboard tail wheel door of the Hansen P-40 restoration carries the autograph of Colonel Robert L. Scott, Jr. whose markings are carried on this P-40E. (Lou Drendel)

The port elevator and stabilizer on the Hansen P-40E. The "tongue" on the elevator is an internal aerodynamic mass balance weight. (Lou Drendel)

The underside of starboard aileron. The small square in the center of the aileron is an of the inspection plates. (Lou Drendel)

LET	PART	LET	PART	LET	PART
A	POSITION TRANSMITTER ACCESS	K	HEATING BOOT ACCESS DOOR	U	FUEL TANK FILLER NECK
B	RADIO ANTENNA	L	STARTER PULL ACCESS DOOR	V	HANDHOLD REINFORCEMENT
C	ANTI-ICER FILLER NECK	M	OIL DRAIN	W	FUSELAGE ACCESS DOOR
D	CABIN CRANK ACCESS DOOR	N	LIFT TUBE	X	HYDRAULIC TANK ACCESS DOOR
E	BRAKE CYLINDER ACCESS DOOR	O	TAIL WHEEL DOOR	Y	INSPECTION DOOR
F	FUSELAGE FOREWARD COVER PLATE	P	TAIL WHEEL ACCESS DOOR	Z	RUDDER HINGE ACCESS DOOR
G	CUNO OIL FILTER ACCESS DOOR	Q	INSPECTION DOOR	AA	CABLE ACCESS DOOR
H	CARBURETOR AIR FILTER	R	COOLANT TANK ACCESS DOOR		
I	PROPELLER BLADE COVER	S	OIL TANK FILLER ACCESS DOOR		
J	PRESTONE AND OIL DRAIN	T	HEATING BOOT DOOR		

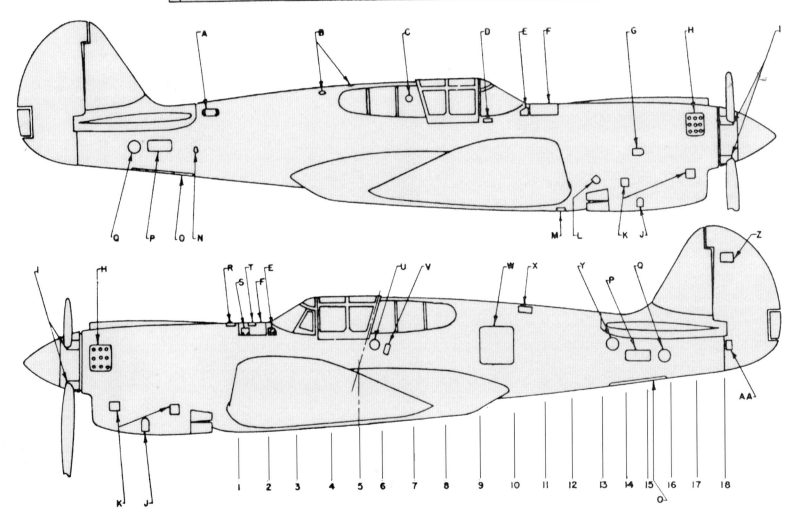

This truck and portable derrick was used by the 49th Fighter Group in Townsville, Australia to perform field maintenance on their P-40Es. Mechanics have removed the entire nose section of a P-40E and placed in in the back of the truck for transport to the repair depot. (Paul Carpenter via Walt Houghton)

Armorers of the 49th Fighter Group clean the six .50 caliber machine guns of a P-40E Warhawk in the shade of the fighter's wing at Townsville, Australia. Curtiss Technical Rep Paul Carpenter is at right. (Paul Carpenter via Walt Houghton)

Maintenance facilities were extremely spartan in the Australian outback, as evidenced by the outdoor overhaul being done on this 49th Fighter Group P-40E. The wing is supported by ropes strung over the trees. (Paul Carpenter via Walt Houghton)

Installation of the Allison V-1710 liquid-cooled engine on the Hansen P-40E installation was accomplished one year prior to the aircraft's first flight. The three radiators are suspended below the engine , with their tubing running back and up to the engine block. (Lou Drendel)

The same Allison V-1710 liquid cooled engine two years after the first flight of the Hansen restoration. The engine has been maintained in almost pristine condition and shows no sign of wear. The heavy tubular engine mounts are in Dark Green. (Lou Drendel)

A P-40E of the 79th Pursuit Squadron, 20th Pursuit Group at Hamilton Field, California during 1941. It carries temporary fuselage markings (cross) applied for pre-war wargames, the group insignia on the fuselage and the squadron insignia on the rudder. (Pete Bowers via Norm Taylor)

This P-40E of the same squadron was on the opposing side and carried different wargame markings on the fuselage and under the wing. (Pete Bowers via Norm Taylor)

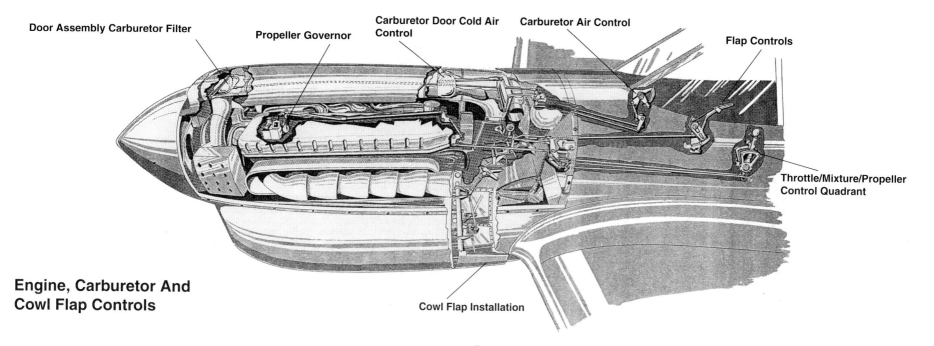

Door Assembly Carburetor Filter

Propeller Governor

Carburetor Door Cold Air Control

Carburetor Air Control

Flap Controls

Throttle/Mixture/Propeller Control Quadrant

Cowl Flap Installation

Engine, Carburetor And Cowl Flap Controls

The Allison V-1710 liquid-cooled inline engine of a P-40E, removed for maintenance. (Paul Carpenter via Walt Houghton)

P-40E radiators. The Glycol coolant radiators are on the left and right, while the slightly smaller oil cooler radiator is in the center. (Lou Drendel)

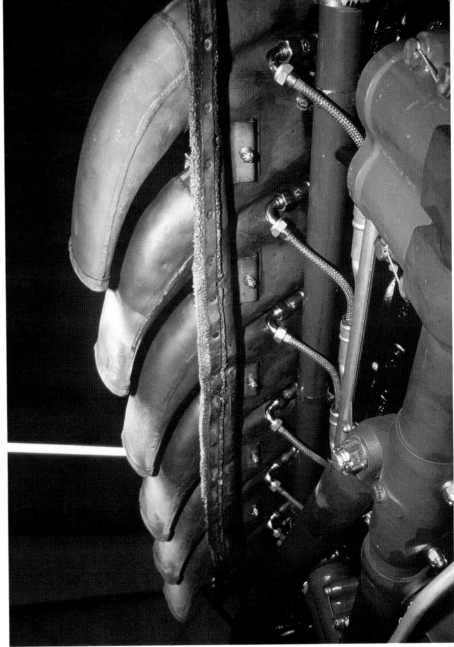

Underside of the Allison V-1710 liquid-cooled engine with the later style exhaust stacks. The six (per side) copper-colored wires are the spark plug wires for the twelve cylinder engine. The engine was rated at 1,150 horsepower at altitude. (Lou Drendel)

There are three cooling radiators for the Allison V-1710 engine. The upper two are for engine coolant, while the lower radiator was the for the oil cooler. (Lou Drendel)

A top view of the Allison V-1710 engine. The Chromate Green tank at the rear is the Coolant Expansion Tank. Just forward of it is the uncovered carburetor air intake. (Lou Drendel)

(Right) The two large Dark Green tubes running along side the engine are the engine mounts , which are anchored to the fuselage bulkhead just forward of the cockpit. The tuned shape of the exhaust stacks is very evident. (Lou Drendel)

This P-40E-1-CU (serial 40-589) of the 344th Fighter Squadron, 343rd Fighter Group, 11th Air Force suffered a "nose bender" at Shemya Army Air Force Base, Alaska on 23 October 1944, when Second Lieutenant Wolf B. Linnemeier landed too fast, applied heavy braking, and nosed over. The aircraft continued to the end of the runway in this attitude bending the propeller blades. Accidents like this were not considered serious by the military, since the pilot often walked away unscathed. The chances were good, however, that the accident resulted in a engine change, since the abrupt engine stoppage probably bent or broke the crankshaft. (Norm Taylor collection)

The upper wing ammunition bay doors were in two parts, a short door and a longer door. Ammunition was loaded into the storage bays through these doors. (via Wayne Fiamengo)

A pristine P-40F Warhawk fresh off the assembly line at Curtiss. The aircraft was built with money donated by the Brotherhood of Railroad Trainmen, and carries their insignia on the nose. This was a very effective method of fund-raising in wartime and the Army Air Force was quick to allow the insignia/logo of the donors organization or names of individuals on the weapons bought with their donations. (Norm Taylor collection)

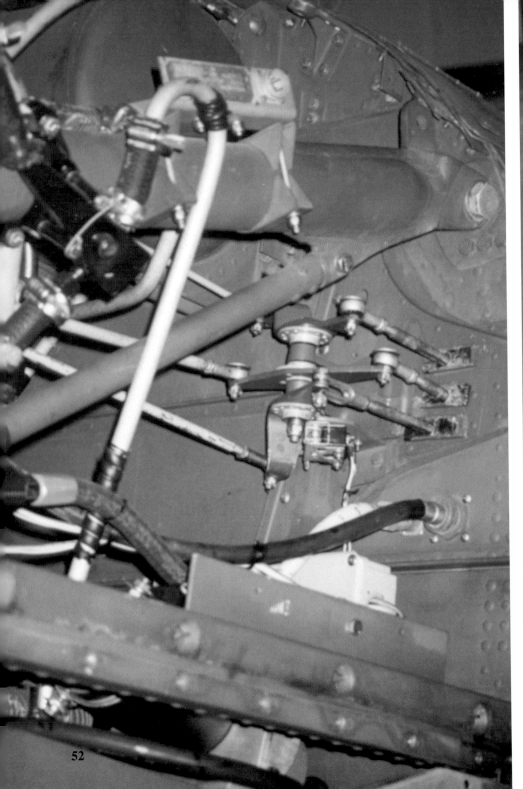

This is the upper starboard side of the P-40E firewall. Just behind the end of the shark-mouth art is the access panel for the engine starter unit. The hole in the wing root is a fresh air intake for the cockpit. (Lou Drendel)

(Left) This is the port side of the P-40E firewall, showing the engine control rods in the center, along with fuel lines (Black) and the upper engine mount. (Lou Drendel)

STARTER

P-40E cooling radiators, with coolent radiators on the top and oil cooler in the center. The engine mount tubing is Dark Green and all the other visible tubes are the plumbing for coolant. (Lou Drendel)

The rear of a V-1710 engine secured to a shipping pallet. (Lou Drendel)

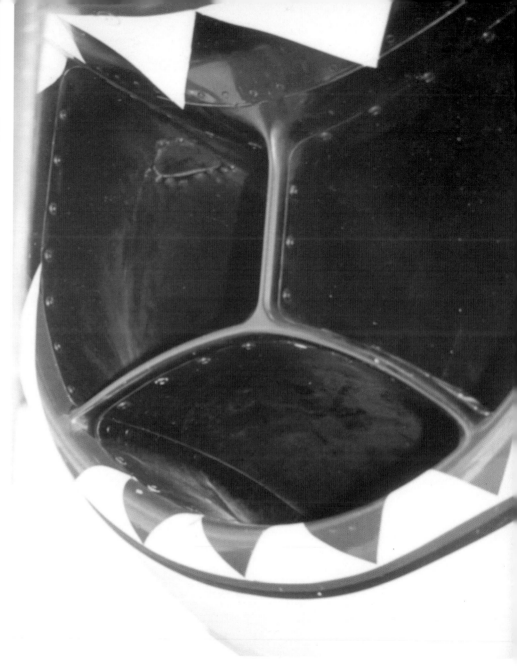

The large nose air intake of the P-40E is devided into three segments to direct air to the three segments of the radiator system. The two upper ducts are much larger than the oil cooler duct. (Lou Drendel)

This P-40K-1-CU (42-46163) came to grief at Shemya AAFB, Alaska on 15 October 1944 when First Lieutenant Britton E. Smith forgot to lower his landing gear. Gear-up landings on PSP (Pierced Steel Planking) often resulted in major airframe damage as the aircraft snagged seams as it slid along. This 344th Fighter Squadron, 343rd Fighter Group Warhawk was a total loss after it's trip down the PSP runway. (Norm Taylor collection)

Shemya was tough on P-40s! Engine failure on takeoff resulted in a stall-spin accident on 13 February 1945. Second Lieutenant Milton D. Cunningham was lucky, he was only at 100 feet when the Allison quit. He was able to walk away from the total wreck of his P-40K-1-CU (serial 42-9865). (Norm Taylor collection)

Battle-damaged flap and upper wing surface of a 49th Fighter Group P-40 shows structural details of the flap panel. (Paul Carpenter via Walt Houghton)

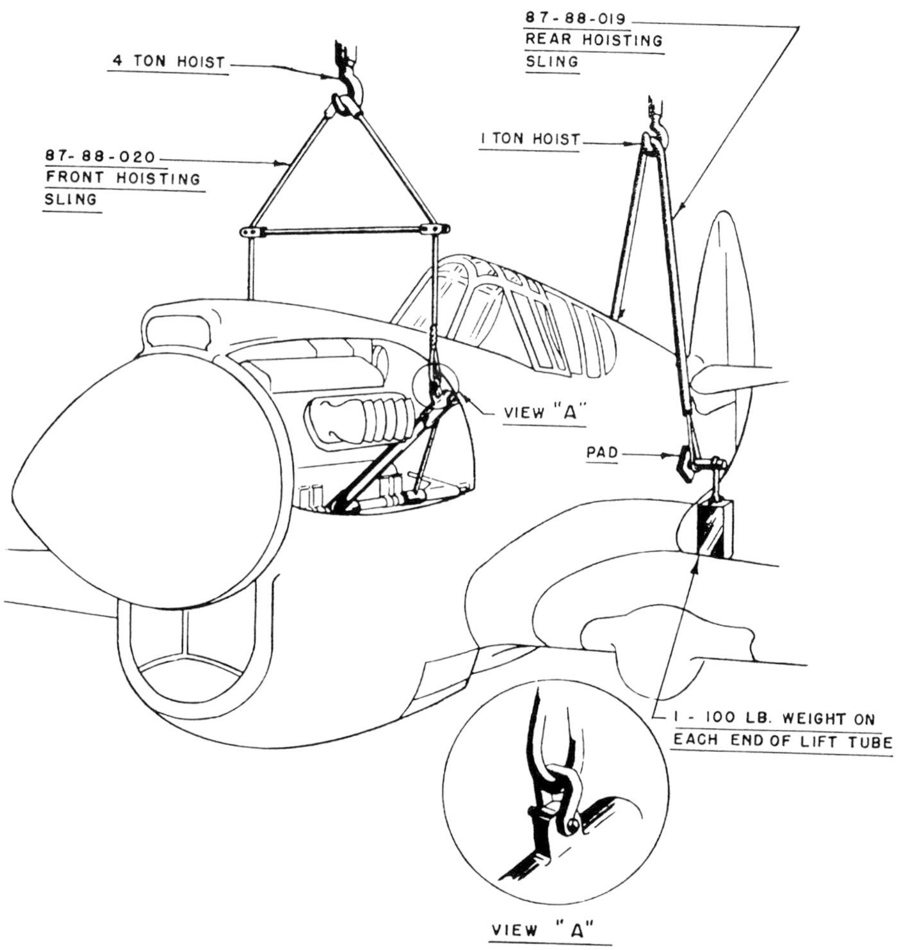
4 TON HOIST
87-88-020
FRONT HOISTING
SLING
87-88-019
REAR HOISTING
SLING
I TON HOIST
VIEW "A"
PAD
I - 100 LB. WEIGHT ON
EACH END OF LIFT TUBE
VIEW "A"

P-40 Hoisting Procedure

This was the method of hoisting the P-40 by crane. It was used on several occasions to load P-40s onto carriers for sea transport to opeational areas, such as the invasion of North Africa.

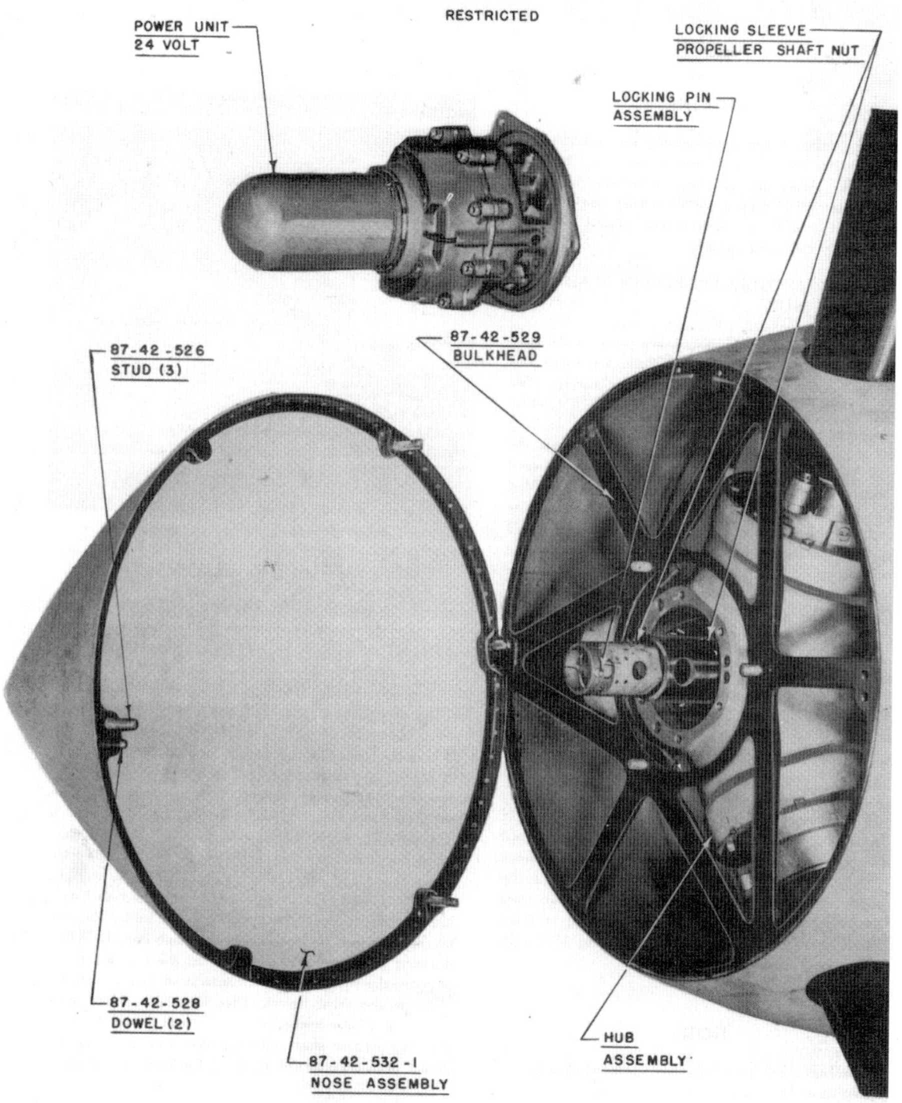
RESTRICTED
POWER UNIT
24 VOLT
LOCKING SLEEVE
PROPELLER SHAFT NUT
LOCKING PIN
ASSEMBLY
87-42-526
STUD (3)
87-42-529
BULKHEAD
87-42-528
DOWEL (2)
87-42-532-I
NOSE ASSEMBLY
HUB
ASSEMBLY

Propeller Spinner and Hub Assembly

Exhaust stack detail on a restored P-40E. This aircraft, like most restored P-40s, used the late style exhaust stacks, instead of the round wartime stacks. (Lou Drendel)

The P-40M differs from the earlier P-40E in that it has a cooling vent on both sides of the nose immediately in front of the exhaust stacks. (Lou Drendel)

The propeller back plate and spinner. Visible inside the acess hole (bottom) in the propeller back plate is the electrical junction to the propeller brush housing. The piping coming down from the engine is the return coolent piping which directs hot coolent back to the radiator system. (Lou Drendel)

Cockpits of the Frasca (left) and Hansen (right) P-40Es show compromises made to be able to use modern avionics (necessary to fly IFR on airways) in the restoration of both aircraft. Both are very authentic, but Frasca has added a modern VHF radio and transponder installed just under the instrument panel, while Hansen hides his modern radios behind a false panel which replicates the old crank handle radios used on the original P-40E on the right cockpit wall. Both have modern VOR/LOC/GS indicators in the instrument panel. (Lou Drendel)

The Allison V-1710 liquid-cooled engine installation in a P-40E. The three radiators abe mounted below the engine with their ducting running off the top of the radiator to the engine. (Lou Drendel)

These are called "Fish Tail" exhaust stacks. Early P-40s had round exhaust stacks, while P-40s beginning with the F variant had the flattened type exhaust stacks. A number of P-40Es were retrofitted with these exhausts. (Lou Drendel)

This RAF Kittyhawk Mk I (P-40E) is equipped with the round type exhaust stacks and a fuselage antenna mast (uncommon on P-40Es). The engine cowl flaps are in the fully open position. (Norm Taylor collection)

Canopy Details

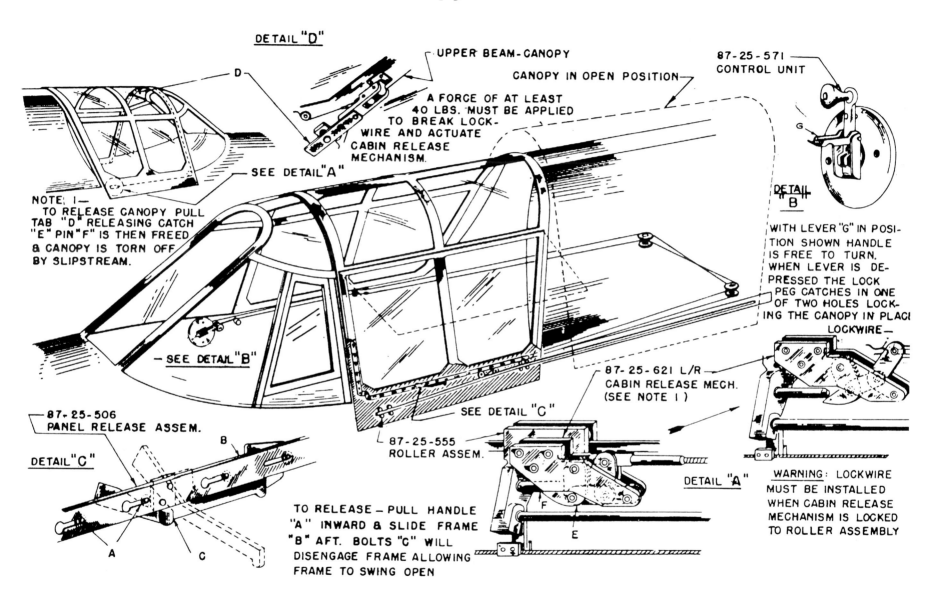

DETAIL "D"

D

SEE DETAIL "A"

NOTE 1—
TO RELEASE CANOPY PULL TAB "D" RELEASING CATCH "E" PIN "F" IS THEN FREED & CANOPY IS TORN OFF BY SLIPSTREAM.

— SEE DETAIL "B"

87-25-506
PANEL RELEASE ASSEM.

DETAIL "C"

B

A   C

UPPER BEAM-CANOPY

CANOPY IN OPEN POSITION

A FORCE OF AT LEAST 40 LBS. MUST BE APPLIED TO BREAK LOCK- WIRE AND ACTUATE CABIN RELEASE MECHANISM.

TO RELEASE — PULL HANDLE "A" INWARD & SLIDE FRAME "B" AFT. BOLTS "C" WILL DISENGAGE FRAME ALLOWING FRAME TO SWING OPEN

SEE DETAIL "C"

87-25-555
ROLLER ASSEM.

F

E

87-25-621 L/R
CABIN RELEASE MECH.
(SEE NOTE 1)

DETAIL "A"

87-25-571
CONTROL UNIT

G

DETAIL "B"

WITH LEVER "G" IN POSI- TION SHOWN HANDLE IS FREE TO TURN. WHEN LEVER IS DE- PRESSED THE LOCK PEG CATCHES IN ONE OF TWO HOLES LOCK- ING THE CANOPY IN PLACE

LOCKWIRE —

WARNING: LOCKWIRE MUST BE INSTALLED WHEN CABIN RELEASE MECHANISM IS LOCKED TO ROLLER ASSEMBLY

The cockpit of a P-40E. The large handle on the right side of the cockpit is the hydraulic pump handle. The interior of the cockpit is Zinc Chromate Green. (Lou Drendel)

Rudy Frasca in the cockpit of his restored P-40E. The rearview mirror above the windscreen was not common on P-40Es, but it was common on all variants after the E. (Lou Drendel)

The headrest in this P-40E is covered in Black leather. The shoulder belt comes over the bar behind the seat. The cushion and backrest were not standard on wartime P-40s. (Lou Drendel)

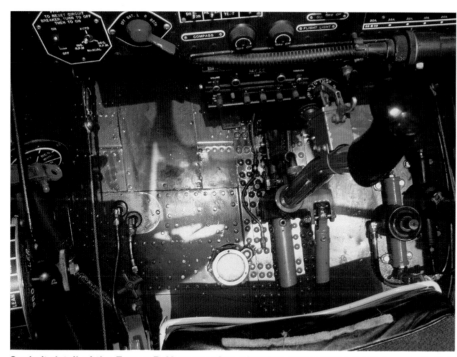

Cockpit detail of the Frasca P-40 restoration, showing connections for the control stick and hydraulic pump handle. (Lou Drendel)

The Black grip on the control stick had a gun trigger switch (Red) and a tailwheel unlock trigger below it in Green. (Lou Drendel)

(Left) The large crank handle opens and closes the sliding canopy. The Red handle to the left is for the engine fire extinguisher. (Lou Drendel)

This P-40L of the 79th Fighter Group in the Western Desert carries five kill markings under the cockpit. This variant of the P-40 had a reflector gunsight and rear-view mirror. (Jim Sullivan collection)

The seat and cockpit floor of a well-used RAAF P-40. (Paul Carpenter via Walt Houghton)

The bullet resistent glass of the windscreen protected the pilot of this P-40 of No. 3 Squadron, RAAF. (Paul Carpenter via Walt Houghton)

RAAF ground crews have patched the battle damage on this P-40 with what appears to be doped fabric. (Paul Carpenter via Walt Houghton)

This two seat conversion of a standard P-40N was designated the TP-40N-30-CU (44-7156). The P-40N was the most numerous version of the series, with 5,219 being built. (Norm Taylor collection)

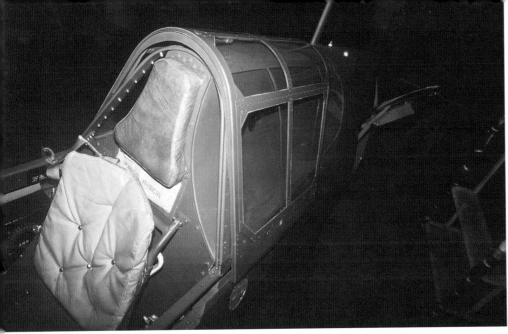

Canopy detail of the Hansen P-40E. The paint on this restored P-40E is more accurate than many other restorations. The headrest is Brown leather, which is closer to wartime P-40s. (Lou Drendel)

The fuselage fuel tank was located immediately behind the pilots seat. Both of the P-40E restorations have fuselage radio antenna masts, which were not used on wartime P-40Es. (Lou Drendel)

The cockpit of the Hansen P-40E showing the port cockpit wall details. The large knobs behind the throttle quadrant control elevator and rudder trim tabs. The lever alongside the seat is used to raise or lower the seat in the cockpit. The hole in the upper section of the instrument panel is where a reflector gun sight was normally installed. (Lou Drendel)

The Hansen P-40E with the stick in full aft position. The round dials on the right canopy rail are the control heads for the original radios. Hansen has concealed a modern circuit breaker panel behind this fold-down display. (Lou Drendel)

The Hansen P-40E was painted in the markings of Colonel Robert Scott and carries authentic kill markings on the fuselage below the cockpit . (Lou Drendel)

Hansen P-40E with the stick in full forward position. The hang-up microphone is authentic, but the radios immediately below and to the left of it are not. (Lou Drendel)

Windscreen and ring gunsight detail on the Hansen P-40E. The P-40E had an armor glass windscreen, (Lou Drendel)

Ground crews work on the engine of this very weathered RAF Kittyhawk in its cotton bale revetment the Western Desert. (Paul Carpenter via Walt Houghton)

The sliding portion of the P-40E canopy. The canopy appears to have been placed on the fuselage and not yet aligned with the canopy track. Also visible is the bracket for a reflector gunsight on the instrument panel. (Lou Drendel)

This is the left side of a P-40E canopy. A Curtiss data plate is mounted under the rear-most fixed canopy glass on both sides. (Lou Drendel)

P-40K-1-CU (42-9987) at the Curtiss factory, 4 November, 1942. The P-40K-1 dfiffered from the earlier P-40K in that it had a longer fuselage and no fin fillet. (Jim Sullivan collection)

A pair of P-40L-20-CUs (serials 42-11081 and 42-11125) fly formation on 30 April 1943. A pair of fairings has been added to the drop tank supports to cut down on drag. (Roger Besecker via Norm Taylor collection)

A P-40E (40-422) of the 79th Pursuit Squadron, 20th Pursuit Group at Oakland Airport, California, during January of 1942. The aircraft has the round style exhaust stacks. (Pete Bowers via Norm Taylor collection)

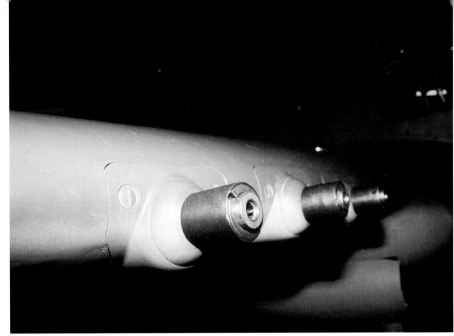

The six wing mounted .50 caliber machine guns on the P-40M have no fairings around the gun ports. (Lou Drendel)

The wing .50 caliber machine guns on the P-40E have a fairing over the gun port. (Lou Drendel)

P-40N of the Confederate Air Force on the ramp at Harlingen, Texas on 24 October, 1971. It carries bogus AVG markings, since the Flying Tigers never flew any variant of the P-40 later than the P-40E. The successor to the Flying Tigers, the 23rd Fighter Group did fly P-40Ks, P-40Ms and P-40Ns. The aircraft also has a modern whip antenna on the fuselage spine (Norm Taylor)

The open P-40E wing gun lower service door. This door was equipped with three ejection slots for the empty .50 caliber shell casings to be ejected overboard. The guns could be checked, removed and reinstalled through this door. Ammunition was loaded from above the wing. (Lou Drendel)

A 100 pound general purpose bomb suspended on the underfuselage bomb rack. The sway braces on either side of the bomb kept it from shifting in flight.

A 300 pound general bomb on the underfuselage bomb rack. This rack could carry up to a 500 pound GP bomb.

RAF Kittyhawks were equipped to carry five 25 pound fragmentation bombs on underwing racks. The small propeller on the nose of the bomb was the arming prop. After a preset number of revolutions, the bomb would be armed. Normally, the props were rendered safe by a safety wire which stayed with the bomb rack when the bomb was released. (Paul Carpenter via Walt Houghton)

This was the 15,000th Curtiss fighter built. The P-40N was given a special paint scheme during November of 1944, with the national insignia of all the countries which used Curtiss aircraft, although not necessarily the P-40. Some of the countries visible are Cuba, China, France, England, Netherlands, Norway, New Zealand, Guatemala, Nicaragua, Turkey, Columbia, Netherlands East Indies, Free French, Portugal and Columbia, with several being repeated. (Via Walt Houghton)

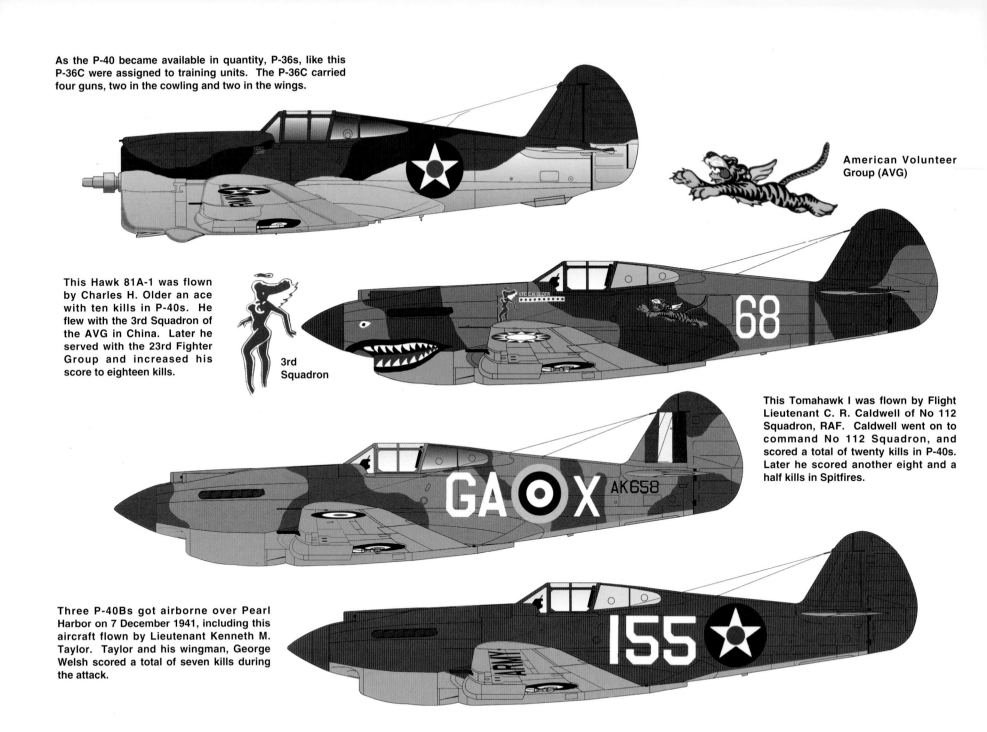

As the P-40 became available in quantity, P-36s, like this P-36C were assigned to training units. The P-36C carried four guns, two in the cowling and two in the wings.

American Volunteer Group (AVG)

This Hawk 81A-1 was flown by Charles H. Older an ace with ten kills in P-40s. He flew with the 3rd Squadron of the AVG in China. Later he served with the 23rd Fighter Group and increased his score to eighteen kills.

3rd Squadron

This Tomahawk I was flown by Flight Lieutenant C. R. Caldwell of No 112 Squadron, RAF. Caldwell went on to command No 112 Squadron, and scored a total of twenty kills in P-40s. Later he scored another eight and a half kills in Spitfires.

Three P-40Bs got airborne over Pearl Harbor on 7 December 1941, including this aircraft flown by Lieutenant Kenneth M. Taylor. Taylor and his wingman, George Welsh scored a total of seven kills during the attack.

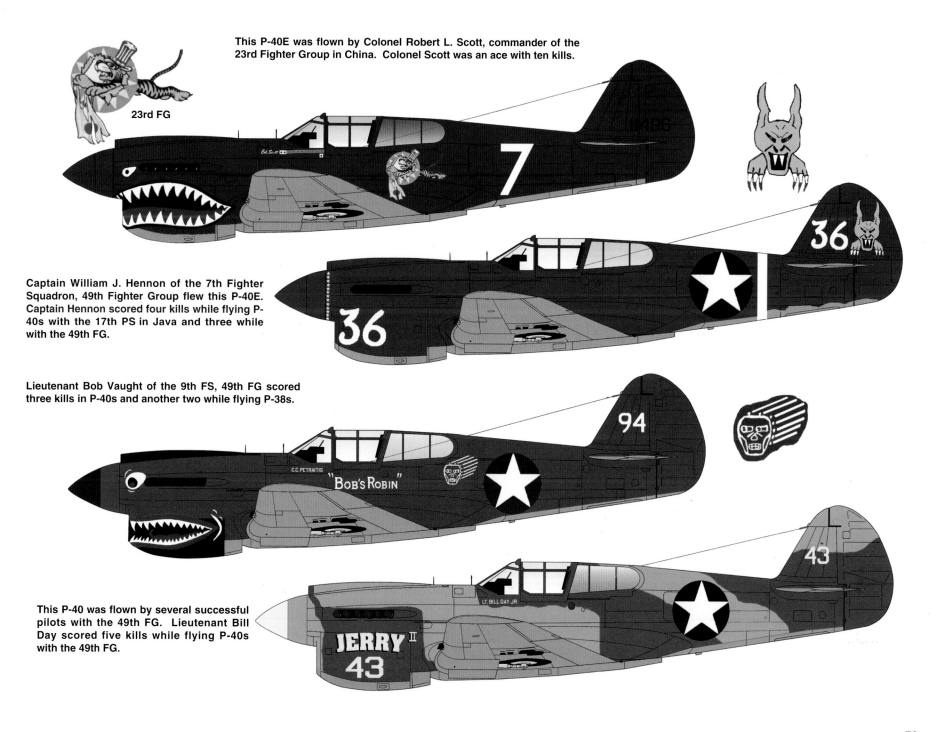

This P-40E was flown by Colonel Robert L. Scott, commander of the 23rd Fighter Group in China. Colonel Scott was an ace with ten kills.

23rd FG

Captain William J. Hennon of the 7th Fighter Squadron, 49th Fighter Group flew this P-40E. Captain Hennon scored four kills while flying P-40s with the 17th PS in Java and three while with the 49th FG.

Lieutenant Bob Vaught of the 9th FS, 49th FG scored three kills in P-40s and another two while flying P-38s.

This P-40 was flown by several successful pilots with the 49th FG. Lieutenant Bill Day scored five kills while flying P-40s with the 49th FG.

This field modified bomb rack on a RAF Kittyhawk I was attached to the standard underfusekage drop tank supports. This field modification was necessary since the Mk 1 did not have a factory installed bomb rack. (Paul Carpenter via Walt Houghton)

Armorer's do maintenance on one of two 50 caliber machine guns carried in the wings of the RAF Tomahawk (P-40B) in the Western Desert during 1941. (Paul Carpenter via Walt Houghton)

Students are shown the workings of a .50 caliber machine gun under the wing of a P-40. There are detached electrical connections hanging from the wing gun bay. (Paul Carpenter via Walt Houghton)

A Curtiss civilian technical representative explains the workings of a .50 caliber machine guns to aviation cadets under the wing of a P-40. (Paul Carpenter via Walt Houghton)

This is the bomb rack installation under the wing of an RAF Kittyhawk. (Paul Carpenter via Walt Houghton)

Armament officers and enlisted men from Orlando, Florida and Charlotte, North Carolina at the Curtiss Wright Corporation Buffalo Plant discuss the armament of the P-40F. This was either pre-war or very early in the war. (Curtiss Wright via Walt Houghton)

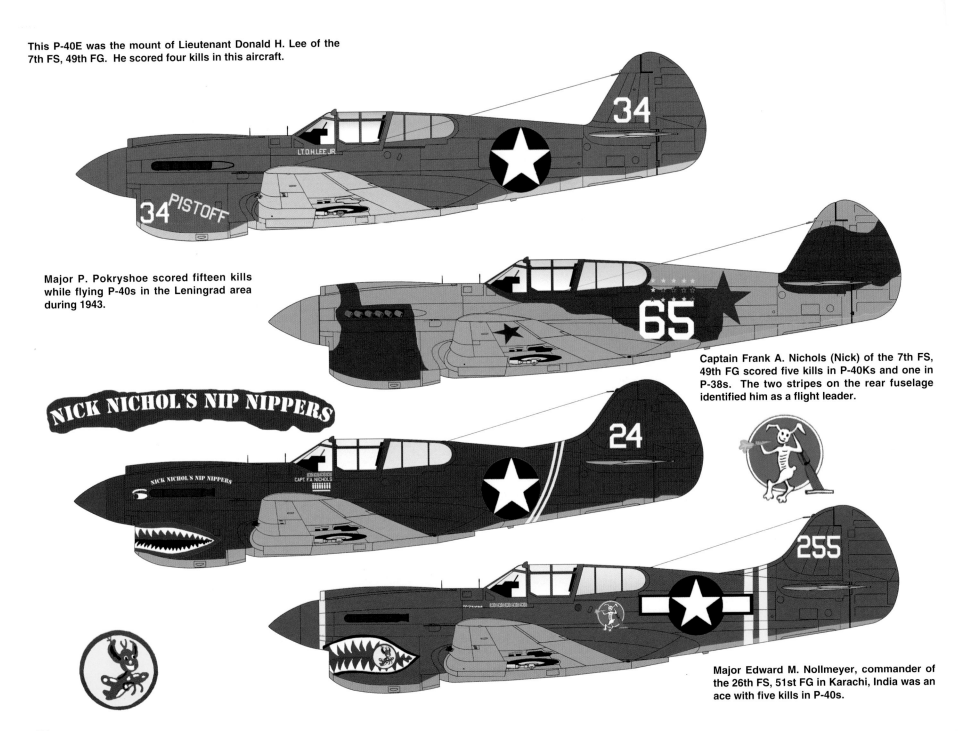

This P-40E was the mount of Lieutenant Donald H. Lee of the 7th FS, 49th FG. He scored four kills in this aircraft.

Major P. Pokryshoe scored fifteen kills while flying P-40s in the Leningrad area during 1943.

Captain Frank A. Nichols (Nick) of the 7th FS, 49th FG scored five kills in P-40Ks and one in P-38s. The two stripes on the rear fuselage identified him as a flight leader.

Major Edward M. Nollmeyer, commander of the 26th FS, 51st FG in Karachi, India was an ace with five kills in P-40s.

Bomb Colors and Markings

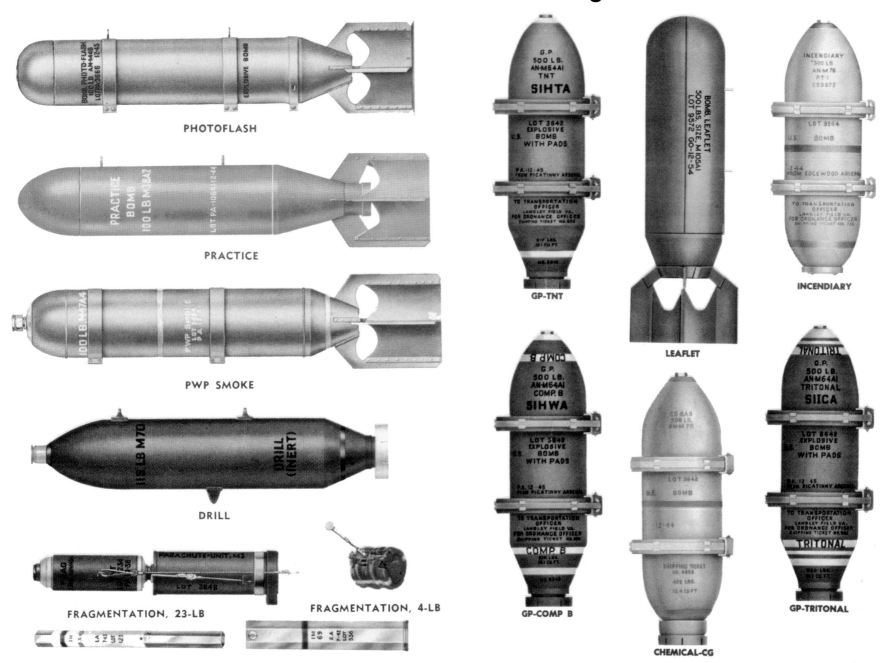

PHOTOFLASH

PRACTICE

PWP SMOKE

DRILL

FRAGMENTATION, 23-LB

FRAGMENTATION, 4-LB

GP-TNT

LEAFLET

INCENDIARY

GP-COMP B

CHEMICAL-CG

GP-TRITONAL

A P-40K (serial 42-46178) launches from USS Breton on 10 December 1943. The use of a catapult launch required modification of the P-40 with the addidition of a hold back cable and catapult bridle. (National Archives via Jim Sullivan)

P-40K (serial 42-46205) launched from USS Breton on 10 December 1943. Additional rudder deflection was required to maintain directional control under the increased power of the improved V-1710-73 engine. (National Archives via Jim Sullivan)

This P-40F (serial 41-14106) was named "IRENE" and was based on Guadalcanal during January of 1943. (F.H. Dixon via Jim Sullivan)

Fewer than two dozen flyable P-40s survive today. This P-40E was photographed at the Talmantz Museum, Orange County, California, during September of 1966. The aircraft was painted in New Zealand markings. (Jim Sullivan collection)

Another civil registered P-40E based in California. This Warhawk was at Oakland, California, during 1962. (Jim Sullivan Collection)

Ex-RCAF P-40E (AL-152 serial 18796) fresh out of the paint shop after its restorataion at Long Beach, California on 7 December 1969. (Tom Piedimonte via Jim Sullivan)

A P-40N-5-CU (serial 42-105927) in bogus AVG markings, looking decidedly derelict at NAS Willow Grove, PA during in 1958, at the dawn of the modern warbird era. This airplane could have been bought for a few thousand dollars then. Today, even in this condition, it would bring hundreds of thousands of dollars. The run-up in warbird prices guarantees that these magnificent airplanes will survive as testaments to one of greatest eras in aviation history. (Bob Esposito via Jim Sullivan)

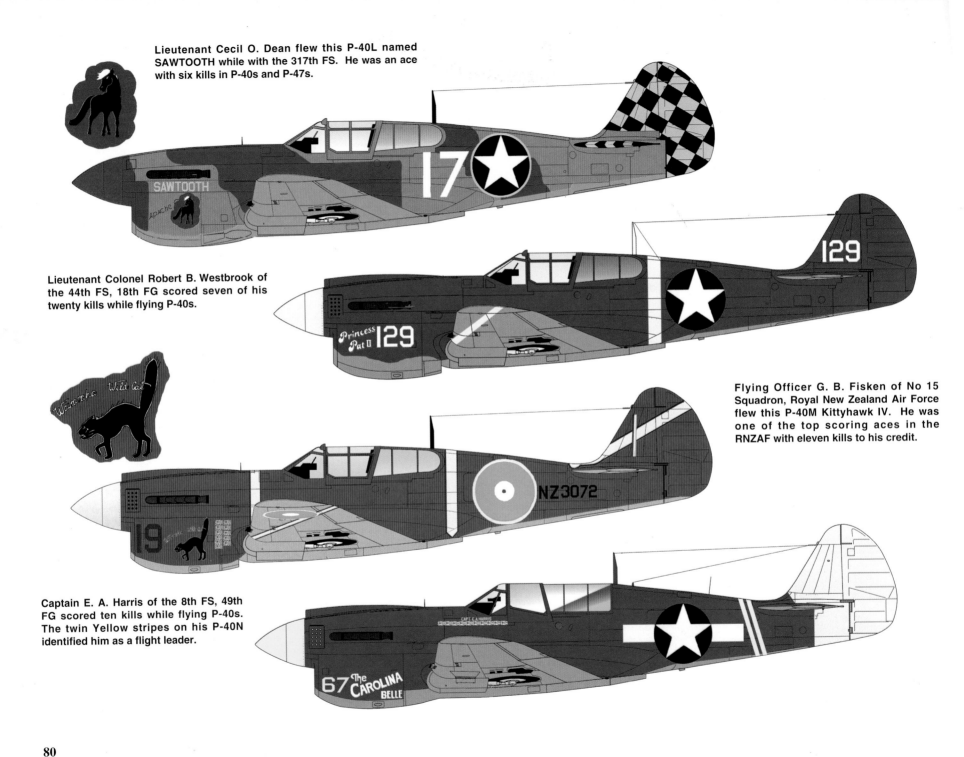

Lieutenant Cecil O. Dean flew this P-40L named SAWTOOTH while with the 317th FS. He was an ace with six kills in P-40s and P-47s.

Lieutenant Colonel Robert B. Westbrook of the 44th FS, 18th FG scored seven of his twenty kills while flying P-40s.

Flying Officer G. B. Fisken of No 15 Squadron, Royal New Zealand Air Force flew this P-40M Kittyhawk IV. He was one of the top scoring aces in the RNZAF with eleven kills to his credit.

Captain E. A. Harris of the 8th FS, 49th FG scored ten kills while flying P-40s. The twin Yellow stripes on his P-40N identified him as a flight leader.